The
Immigration
Handbook

D1100035

for Barry

The
Immigration
Handbook

Caroline Smith

Seren is the book imprint of
Poetry Wales Press Ltd.
57 Nolton Street, Bridgend, Wales, CF31 3AE
www.serenbooks.com
facebook.com/SerenBooks
twitter@SerenBooks

The right of Caroline Smith to be identified as
the author of this work has been asserted in accordance
with the Copyright, Designs and Patents Act, 1988.

© Caroline Smith 2016

ISBN: 978-1-78172-321-0
ebook: 978-1-78172-322-7
Kindle: 978-1-78172-323-4

A CIP record for this title is available from the British Library.

All rights reserved. No part of this publication may be reproduced,
stored in a retrieval system, or transmitted at any time or by any means,
electronic, mechanical, photocopying, recording or otherwise without
the prior permission of the copyright holder.

The publisher acknowledges the financial assistance of the Welsh Books Council.

Cover Artwork: 'Panel 57: the female workers were the last to arrive north, 1940-41'
copyright Estate of Jacob Lawrence. ARS, NY and DACS, London 2015.

Printed in Bembo by Bell and Bain Ltd, Glasgow

Whilst the lives represented in these poems reflect actual events and
experiences, all names have been changed and no individual is identifiable.

BRENT LIBRARIES	
91120000347139	
Askews & Holts	18-Oct-2017
821.92	£9.99

Contents

'It reduces the weight otherwise to be accorded to the requirements of firm and fair immigration control, if the delay is shown to be the result of a dysfunctional system which yields unpredictable, inconsistent and unfair outcomes.'

– Lord Bingham

I have found myself judge in the Court of King Shahrayar
A thousand and one tales of despair poured before me
From an un-stoppered jar
Stories of perilous journeys made over desert sands
Of palaces that rise up overnight only to disappear at dawn
A speaking bird serves a dish of cucumbers stuffed with pearls
This woman with no documents has only the eloquence of her words

On Hold

'There is no timescale for dealing with this application.'

He was just twenty-three,
Arjan Mehta, when first he began
calling the Home Office
from a red phone box
on the corner of Preston Road;
would push against
and let fall behind him
the heavy creaking door,
into its stale, vacated, smoke smell,
stand on its concrete, littered floor
his fingers twisting through
the plastic snake cord,
dragging round the metal dial,
eager about his application.
Seventeen years have passed
with no answer.
He is now forty.
The sealed-up phone box
long out of service,
the black cradle
within its sepulchre,
silent as an obsidian urn.

The Boxer

As if I've moved a board from the grass
and uncovered white, straggly, bolted strands,
this one-time Russian boxer
has emerged after years of hiding.

His nose undulates, the tip protruding
from his flattened face, his pallid skin shows
the scars of fights and drifting,
as he gesticulates the story of his last fight

in 1997 against Gary Stone-Face Henderson –
former middleweight champion –
a warm-up act in a half-full, blue-lit arena
an unequal contest he couldn't win.

How, as his gumshield was removed
and water splashed over his swollen head
and as the crowd surged to its feet roaring
the entrance of the hero on the main bill,

he had slipped away from his minders
his fixers and the restrictions of his visa
into the urban undergrowth of bus shelters,
the shredded hessian of unlocked sheds.

Somewhere in the damp holds of the Home Office
a scrap of paper with his name was lost,
overlain with the heavy files of newer conflicts
and the years, like a soothing poultice,

began to break down his identity,
braille his documents with mildew and
the wet, black gills of fungus; crumble
the pages into the soil he's become a part of.

The Scarlet Lizard

Nothing moves
except the evening light
crossing the Judge's room.
The lawyers' skeleton arguments
lay piled on his desk.
They seemed to him brittle
as bleached poppies,
tapped of their seeds.

He longed to see the quick movement
of a scarlet lizard weaving unexpectedly
through the parched, cracked hexagons
of a legal phrase, to hear the snapped stick
fritter away from a hiding place;
to feel the cold, diaphanous weed grip
in the black current of a border crossing.

He needed to sense some quiver of
indecision, an odd detail
that would open the truth of their words;
chinks of light shining
through shuttered doors.

Lime Tree Honey

The regulation for Citizenship demands proof that an applicant was in the UK exactly five years before the date of application.

All she had brought with her
from that other life in the DDR
was a dill pickle jar filled with honey
made by his bees, from trees
in the Unter den Linden.
It would remain unopened,
a jar of time that could not change
but that preserved one day in their life together
as she had decided to remember it.

The honey held the burnished light
of an early morning leaving East Berlin
to take the swarm to the countryside
to pollinate an orchard.
It held the cobbled roads of the hamlets
they had meandered through:
the scent of flowering beans
through the open windows,
stalks of chaff that blew round the car,
the back of the old hatchback
bumping and scraping low behind them
with the packed hives, shifting –
and the restless hum of the bees.

In the shock that had enveloped her
after the release of her file
and the discovery of her husband's
meticulous notes on her life,
she had searched back
as she prepared to leave Germany
for signs of his affection –
some drop of sweetness
she could extract from those years.

I.S 96

The refusal notice told him he was
'Appeal rights exhausted'. He was.
After eleven years on Temporary Admission,
like a shipwrecked survivor
staggering up the shore,
he had collapsed on the tide's edge
to the boom of the sea
and the cry of the gulls.
With each new refusal
he'd felt the sinking pull and roll
of pebbles shifting beneath him
dragging him back out to sea.
But as year followed year and
they never made him leave,
his fragile hope took root, lacing
the bleached crowns of matted grass
to the quiet leeside of the dunes
among the flat, violet stones
and brittle bundles of seaweed
that drifted across the paths
of half-buried sleepers.

Brook Court

The paunch of the gas fire blows and pops.
Residents are slumped in their high seats
beneath the cross of Jesus/Lakshmi with four arms.

There's a smell of hot static age in the tumble drier.
The fridge hums, shuddering into a quiet period.
Anne-Marie swings back chrome lids whose insides run with water.

Mrs Kaminski remembers a banquet in Krakow;
a row of waiters standing, one hand behind their backs,
percussionists lifting silver domes.

Mrs Kaminski had three governesses —
each to speak to her in a different language —
she wishes one had been Filipino.

In the dark chapel
Anne-Marie prays to the Madonna
to get legal, to see her children again.

Ninety-eight-year-old Mr Gosar-Shah was her first chance.
For seven months, she bathed his quivering, soft-splattered skin,
emptied the blood-orange spume of his catheter bag;

blurting out the wet-nosed tube of his cream,
which scurried and tumbled,
a small white animal darting from its hole.

He died two weeks before her appeal
and she no longer had a case. But she searched
and found Mrs Kaminski — only eighty-seven.

Outside snow dries into a crystalline crust.
Mrs Kaminski worries Anne-Marie doesn't see the warnings;
that she'll be taken away in a raid.

Mrs Kaminski worries she will sit all day in her crumpled nightdress,
white legs over the side of the bed, sun splashing
silently through the curtains, still drawn at noon.

Teenager

The only thing he remembered
about the burglary was the dog
as he'd dragged it across the floor,
its claws out in resistance,
fur hooding its eyes.
His own teeth were bared
as he shook and twisted
the folds of its neck.
The dream of his father!
His mute mother
had brought him here to
join him and he'd found
a drunk, violent man
who beat her.
He knew at court, that he
had an extra punishment.
He would be deported when
the others were released.
At the time he didn't care,
he hated this shit-hole of a country
as much as it hated him.
But inside, he found
he was good at maths,
got certificates in fitness,
reflected on his life.
But it was down in writing
that he hated his mother
so now they said he hadn't
got family life.
He'd told them he was glad
he'd hurt the dog
so they said he had no remorse.

They told him he was now
nineteen and no longer a child
and would be deported with £46.
They asked him which airport
he wanted to go back to
but he didn't know
what ones there were.
He'd left when he was seven.

Eaton House

Dr Khan has been walking for seven years
out to Hounslow to join the queue
and each week sign his name.
He edges forward, his face burning
as if he's standing in the market place
of his home in Paktika Province.
Word has got back from new arrivals.
'Even Dr Khan is in the queue with us.
He told his wife he was practising in England.'

Every week he has described for her
the life he is building.
She imagines the slow, steep climb
up to the pass
the sun rising over the next ridge
where he can see the summit
the skylarks veering from the scrub
into blue sky – the crossing point
where he's gone too far to turn back.

Citizenship Ceremony

Every few months a timetable clash
means the Citizenship Ceremony
and the asylum surgery converge.
From outside the council chamber,
as each new citizen is made,
we can hear the patter of applause.
It is rain to parched, thirsty soil —
every head turns and lifts
towards the sound.

Luck

A sudden deep snowfall
has grounded all flights.
Mr Owusu's deportation,
that we've fought so hard against,
is unexpectedly cancelled.
Our faces are grey and wrinkled
against the brightness of snow.
Boots creak and squeal in the thick silence
as we decide to walk these country lanes,
quiet again as when my mother and her father,
evacuees from the bombs of London,
once cycled under the jumbled hedgerows
alive with birds and berries –
heading for the canal –
fishing rods strapped to their backs.
One day they caught a large perch
and wrapped it in wet newspaper
to take back for supper.
She carried it in her basket
for the long cycle home.
It was still alive when they got there
to their rooms above the Post Office –
where my mother, afraid to sleep,
would read under the street light.
They put the perch in the sink
and the next day
cycled all the way back to the canal
and let it go.
They figured it had somehow
deserved its luck.

Selection

He was quietly hopeful
when he got the letter
that said his case had been
'selected for progression',
that he would be allowed to stay.
But then a second had arrived:
'an invitation to a service event'
and he was suspicious.
Too much activity –
this sudden attention to him.
He was scared.
It was as if after all these
years of hiding, he would,
finally be led out with the
other men and boys,
through the fringe of sunlight
from the gloom of the pine forest
his hands clasped behind his head.

Red Road Flats

When the Presenting Officer heard of
their suicides following the ruling
it was as if he'd woken up
and found himself
a trespasser in his own garden.
He read back through the files
began to doubt his own certainty.
What he had dismissed as paranoid, he
now saw from within their world as real,
not benign, not to be trusted,
just as an early morning frost brings out
a previously invisible conspiracy of
white cobwebs connecting the grasses.

The Pilgrimage

As he looked through cases
he often wondered if his own life
could withstand such scrutiny.
Now checking this man's documents
for illegal working,
he notes the withdrawal of £5 each Friday night
from a cashpoint in Norwich, at the end of a week
lifting heavy turkeys in the meat plant –
before returning to a caravan
he shares with seven others –
his balance: £3.92 at the end of six months.

He felt reluctance, superstition almost
to decide this case. The man had been
picked up by immigration on a pilgrimage.
He must have known there was a chance
officers would be waiting –
they had last year – but the man
had gone anyway.
And now he felt, not so much
that he was being asked to weigh up
this man's life, but that somehow he
himself was being judged – still
being judged for what he'd done 20 years ago,
when as a young, drunken farmer in Łodz
he'd stepped outside the boundaries
of his own faith
and created his future.
But there again without the drink
he might never have done it –
never have got talking to a Westerner –
might still be on the farm
slopping swill across the cobbled yard

to the shrieking, whinnying piglets
pummelling at the teats of the slumped
exhausted sow –
couldn't now even if he wanted to,
return like some prodigal son, all forgiven –
there was no farm to go back to,
he'd sold it that night
for enough dollars to buy a coach ticket out.

But sometimes at night, he heard
the tick of insects in the long bleached grass
creeping gradually over the yard,
saw the door hanging off the wooden pen,
felt the lightness of the dollars in his hand,
the empty space in his life where the pigs had lain,
solid as boulders along the ledges of shade,
sunken eyes under curled, laurel-veined ears
their chestnut hair glinting through cracked, olive mud
like the copper reliquaries of his faith.

The Jumper

She remembered those first weeks
training as a nurse in a foreign land –
homesick, cold.
How she missed her family.
How she had been tempted:
all the colours,
beautiful designs
and how she'd slipped one into her bag.
How she'd been caught,
but thought the Judge had been kind.
How her family had come to join her –
their excitement,
their first days at school.
How they had flourished.
How she never told them.
How she'd forgotten
until now, when the letter came
refusing them all
because of her criminal act.
How she couldn't explain to her children.
How she could see no other way –
how without her, they'd be allowed
to stay.

Asylum Documents

He thought the electronic records
had made him more detached.
There was something about
handling their scraps of documents
that had touched him:
the worn, felted papers
rubbed through in damp pockets
the letters from home,
the photographs fused together
into hard, cracked tiles
the pages that rose and fell
under his hands.
It was like turning the leaves of
his wife's grease-stained cook book
with the yellow, brittle, Sellotape,
her smudged, sloping hand.
From them he could remember
every recipe she'd cooked him
all the meals they'd shared.

Mrs Shah's Complaint

It was as if she'd toiled to the top
of a mountain
only to find that day trippers
on their coaches, with picnics and cokes,
had found a road up the other side.

The Administrative Removal Officer

My hands have grown tough and split
from the twisted ground I work in;
prising off vines locked round fences,
cutting back branches,
pulling away armfuls of climbers.
Purple worms recoil from me
twisting into figures of eight
my feet crush sickly-pale apricot snails
sheltering in the damp pelts
of wet undergrowth.
I lever back my fork
and hear the snap and resistance of roots.
I must clear this plot
steel my heart to dig up
perfect flowers in full bloom.

Jozef Rexha – salesman

He'd sold a vacuum cleaner today
for £2,500 to a Brenda Watts.
Took five hours to get her to sign.
He'd even opened up her old one for her
showed her it was blocked.

As he'd lifted off the heavy lid
and pulled out a trunk of matted dust
he'd caught the haze of pine needles –
the back of a cart piled with fresh-chopped trees
in a frost-hard courtyard at dusk.
He remembered the monastery,
the Trappist monks with their felt boots
tramping over silver snow in the blue twilight.
Silent, obsessed with the quality of sound
and snared like him in an urgent world
of signs and whispers:
the rumour of a queue forming
that would flash across the village
like the creak and stretch of a foot on ice.

He did pity the old woman.
Knew how she'd feel when she closed her door
on the soundproofed, deadened stairway.
The huge disappointment, her fear,
her sense of falling.

Judicial Consideration

In front of me is an Arrest Warrant, poorly typed
and a Diploma, neither on headed paper.
Both documents have the same dropped g and
the same large gap between lower case i when
it's followed by a lower case c.
I have considered whether two typists could,
randomly, have made the same spacing error
using two different typewriters, and excluded
that possibility. I have also considered whether
the poor public services complained of by the
Appellant could have led the Chief Prosecutor's
Office and the University of Tirana to share the
same worn out typewriter and I must exclude
that possibility as well.

Settlement

He steered the wheelbarrow
of damp mowings
round the bend in the garden path.
Always there,
in the corner of his eye
the cankerous pelt of the compost heap
pressed through the wire mesh cage.
Like a heavy-shouldered bison
it had leaned its depressed weight
against him for nine years.
He stabbed his fork
into the dark overhang,
just as a break in the cloud,
like a token of grace,
rippled over its back.
It lifted him momentarily
like the rumour of the amnesty had
when for weeks he imagined he already
held the document in his hands –
flimsy hearsay that had filled out
the muscles of his dreams,
set a million buffalo
pounding the vast prairies again.

Delay

Home Office

UK Visas and Immigration
PO Box 3468
Sheffield
S3 8WA
Tel
Fax On Request
Email
Web www.gov.uk/uk-visas-immigration

Our Ref

Your Ref

Date   21 September 2015

Dear Sirs

Re:

I refer to your clients No Time Limit application which has been outstanding since 12 December 2006.

I apologise for the delay in progressing your clients application.

Due to the length of time that has elapsed since your client submitted her application the form is now out of date.

I would be grateful if you could download the current NTL form from our website and send it to me using the enclosed envelope. Your client is NOT required to submit any further fee with the application form.

Once the completed form is received I will forward you a letter for your client to register her biometric information for a biometric residence permit.

Yours faithfully

LIVSET 5

Home Office

on behalf of the Secretary of State

Encs:

Pro Bono 1

This woman's only child was killed
as they fled Kosovo and he, a lawyer,
is preparing her asylum appeal.
In the midday office heat
keyboards click like cicadas on sun-baked tiles.
As a door opens then closes he hears
a brief murmuring of hooded voices
and he could be in a Florentine Monastery
crossing a quiet courtyard
unlocking the door to the Scriptorium.

Sometimes he sees himself
as an Illuminator of Letters,
this folio he is crafting, a miniature
of Mary at the foot of the cross.
He paints the shade of the dimpled olive grove,
the sudden stillness,
just the beating throat of a salamander
poised on a rock in the dusty heat,
the drapery of the woman's back
frozen into stone.

Like the choice of lapis used sparingly
for the moment of revelation,
he must place words carefully:
uncover details, minute inflections
that will capture her suffering, unique
on a template of ancient sorrows.

Pro Bono 2

He is looking at her image
from his case file, struggling to find
the truth of this woman's situation,
the argument that will sway the Judge.
She is no longer at risk in Kosovo
but she's established her life here now
and cannot bring herself to return
to the country that killed her son.

In the smoke-dry heat of the office,
he allows his mind to drift like wild lavender
outside the margins of the page –
thinking of the medieval illuminators,
a lifetime studying their craft.
They too found the conventions lacking
the rules they had inherited, made for a different age,
began to alter perspective,
and find different ways to represent truth.

If he is to capture the complexities of this woman's case
it will not be in the accuracy of her likeness;
painting the bullet holes in the belfry
where a sniper once positioned himself
above the silver-grey olive grove
climbing the hillside;
it will be in the beauty of his argument
the legal arabesques that cut across borders,
extending the picture beyond its frame.

Fault Line

When his parents met in South Africa
how were they to know that fifty years later
their son, with two names, would need to
reconcile them on an EU Residence card.
That there would be nowhere on the form to explain
why they had to move to Swaziland
and register his birth at the Portuguese Consulate
in his father's name and when the work permit
ran out, no choice but to go back,
a mixed-race couple to South Africa
where his mother would give him her name
and an Identity card where 'Father'
was left blank.

Tangiers

Cyril B has fallen out with Cyril M.
He will be persuaded to make up only
if he is sure Cyril M really is dying this time.
They sing *Onward Christian Soldiers*
from maroon hymnbooks,
the tissue thin pages of Ancient & Modern,
in a whitewashed church, alongside
Liberians waiting to cross to Europe.
Two hundred and twenty ex-pats
still live in Tangiers.
One hundred and six asylum seekers
died last year trying to cross the
eight miles the other way to Spain.

Cyril B's socks are on display:
one yellow, one cumin-brown
extended for Mahmood to swish brushes,
sleek as otter pelts, over the toe caps.
The popped-off tin lids of Oxblood
polish lie open in a wooden box
like stippled, rain-soaked Fenlands –
with Cambridge spires,
where Mahmood dreams of studying
and Cyril B has left behind –
but still goes back to buy his shoes.

Mahmood posts cigarette butts
into an empty Sprite bottle
that glistens in the heat.
The watches round the arm of a vendor
catch the light – it's the same light
that in the mornings
plays through the window
of Cyril B's bedroom onto the mirror,
mottled orange and silver like a plaice,
where he sleeps with the ashes of his father
in an urn under the bed.

Mahmood spent twelve years in England
hiding in a caravan with fruit pickers,
vacating it when the farmer needed it
to mate one of his dogs. He remembered
the rain-grey fruit fused to the stems,
the day they lifted the grain bin and
found a nest of purple ratlings:
the mother had clung to a stick
but the greyhound snapped it in half.
He had almost made it to fourteen years,
when they'd have given him his papers,
let him stay –
but he'd got a message from home
that his mother was dying –
and he'd had to choose.

Spouse Visa

Her hands churn up the muddy sink,
rub at thin skins of small potatoes that
nose and flutter against her searching fingers,
wrapping around her in silky lace.
She had wanted to believe him,
her young Turkish prince, when he told her
that he'd first fallen in love with her hands;
and the glimpse of pale arm that slipped out
from under her Harris tweed.

She hadn't been back on the rota to help
since he'd left her.
She knew she'd been foolish
but she'd signed his papers anyway.
Because for two years
she had been the moon's grace,
had shed the wrinkles of her old age,
seen her body emerge nubile and beautiful,
gleaming as newly washed sand.

Removal

I watch the clock all day
as it edges nearer
to the time of your deportation.
The flurry of faxes and
pre-action protocol interventions
have stilled
as it becomes clear
removal will proceed.
A silence hangs over Yarl's Wood.
Practical arrangements are put in motion.
The life support around you
has been taken away.

Valerie

She was agitated.
She should have dressed up for him last night.
It was his birthday. He'd asked her to
but she'd refused and he'd got upset
and gone out
didn't come back until the morning.
She should have dressed up:
he could dump her, send her back.
She jerked the buggy wheels
swivelling into the corner
as the baby began to snore
through its cleft palate,
dummy balanced on its lip,
thin sky-blue hood
pulled over its eyes.

She hadn't known she had no visa
until she witnessed a fight and came forward;
she ended up being the one arrested!
Just a kid she was when she'd come.
Her auntie had arranged it.
Thought she was coming to school
but ended up slaving for the family.
Auntie kept her passport
but didn't do nothing about her stay.
An elder at the church had given her the eye.
She'd wanted to make something of her life
but it turned out it was the only way.

Answer Machine

The answer machine messages
collect through the night,
brim like the water butt
spilling over with black water.

Apology

I apologise to both you and Ms Bensoussan that we have previously provided you with inaccurate information about her case. I would also apologise that Ms Bensoussan's case has not been correctly routed within this office, and for the delay that this has caused.

As representations made under an enforcement policy, any consideration of Ms Bensoussan's case should have fallen to her local Immigration Compliance and Engagement (ICE) team to deal with, but officers from our former Case Resolution Directorate (CRD) appear to have incorrectly taken action on her case. The residual functions of our former CRD were later taken over by our former Case Assurance and Audit Unit, and which is now known as the Older Live Cases Unit (OLCU). It was realised that Ms Bensoussan's case should not have been with the OLCU at the time of our reply to you of 4 January 2012, and with our reply of 9 January 2012 being an error. Our response of 14 June 2012 to your letter of 30 May 2012 correctly advised you that Ms Bensoussan's case had been transferred to our Sheffield casework area, although I am sorry that the statement that Ms Bensoussan would be contacted within 28 days was over optimistic. In retrospect Ms Bensoussan's application should not have been passed to our Sheffield casework area, which mainly deals with charged applications, given that she had not made such an application. This appears to be a further consequence of Ms Bensoussan's case being incorrectly recorded as an "application" on our computer system.

Ms Bensoussan's Home Office file did reach our Sheffield casework area in August 2012, although it was later transferred back to the OLCU in October 2012 as our Sheffield casework area considered that it was not for them to deal with. Your enquiries of 3 September 2012, 8 October and 21 November 2012 were all noted on Ms Bensoussan's computer record, although I am sorry that this did not result in her case being concluded. Ms Bensoussan's file was subsequently sent back to our Sheffield casework area in January 2013, after your office spoke with Yvonne Walton of this office.

Judgements

"I as an Adjudicator must only exclude matters
from consideration if I have no real doubt that they
did not occur. Similarly if the appellant claimed
that relevant matters did not happen I should not
exclude the possibility that they did not happen
(although believing that they probably did)
unless I had no real doubt that they did in fact happen."

The Strange Tale of the Immigration Judge & the Carpet Seller of Kampala

It had been a long day in Court;
dispensing justice, despatching lives
and as the Judge hurried home through
the deepening light, he found the curious
case of Harun al Rashid following him.
At the time he had given little credence
to the story. A careless Clerk had just
spilt coffee down his robes.
He had dismissed the case and sacked the Clerk,
but now as the world began to lose its shape,
the day's hearing pushed through
his crowded thoughts and he found
the persistent figure of Harun al Rashid
had returned to insist on a proper hearing.

A case lost in the archives of Home Office time,
the appeal form claimed that Harun al Rashid
was a 'twilight operative'
living at Unit Three, The Industrial Estate.
But something in his proud bearing
brought to mind his noble namesake,
the great Haroon Er-Rasheed,
Khaleefah of all Persia.

This Rashid claimed to be a carpet seller by trade,
to have once been the respectable owner
of a beautiful, if sprawling emporium.
It was a casket of silks conjured
from a war-torn land,
exotic carpets of every hue and weave
samples white as pure unrolled snow,
persimmon rugs with the spring of impala
all shamelessly displayed
like the tool of a lively mule.
And in his brief Court appearance
the Judge had seen that the man's stiff fingers,
splayed-out like a cockerel tail,
still remembered the pride of holding
a colourful swatch between them.

43

Rashid's troubles had begun long ago
when in kindness he had taken into
his shop a young apprentice.
In later years, he would rehearse
the months the boy had spent with him,
would wake wondering if he had
failed to tack a runner to a stair
so that the boy's feet had cart-wheeled
down a revolving belt of looped pile.
Or had he scolded him
for being too extravagant with the underlay?
He would flick round tombolas
of twists and tweeds,
of weights and equations
always asking how the timid boy
he had known could have become such a tyrant.
But finally he had to conclude
that he lived in a capricious world,
where what appears good fortune turns out bad
and what bad, can in the end come good.

It was many years after the apprentice
had left his employ, now risen
to the rank of General and ruler of the land,
that the night of Rashid's downfall began.
The palace servants were making final,
frenzied plans for a visit of State.
And as the General strolled the sweeping hallways
marvelling at his lavish splendour, he noticed
a mark on the carpet no bigger than a shred of yam.
He flew into a quivering rage
and ordered the carpet be ripped up
and a new one laid that very night.
It was Harun al Rashid's ill-fated name
that came to mind and he was summoned.

Truth to tell Rashid at first was flattered.
He chose his finest, his most exquisite silk.
He crawled on his knees,
cutting and splicing, stretching and tacking
so that when he had finished,

the carpet shimmered
like spools of golden jinneeyeh.
The General was delighted,
but instead of a reward
of priceless treasure, he ordered
the other thirty rooms of his palace
to be laid with the same silken thread.
And before dawn broke, or be
thrown into a jail with no key.

Harun al Rashid called in every favour
from every eager young bachelor he
had ever lent an offcut of flecked twill
to entice a bride over a threshold.
Weavers squatted, wheels turned,
shuttles flew, feet pedalled,
the bolts of silken carpet slid from the
bamboo looms and were lifted by
a chain of porters through the streets.
All night Harun al Rashid fitted carpet
until dawn lifted its cruel blade
and he crept to his ruined emporium,
his fingers locked wide as camel saddles,
his back broken. That night he fled.

By morning the tired Judge
was still pondering the unlikely story
he had been told by the carpet seller
from Kampala and the ill-fortune
of his strange commission.
Now he realised that in his haste
to dismiss the Appeal
he had overlooked
one important detail:
the name of this apprentice, Idi.
The Judge dressed quickly
and hurried back to the Court room
resolved to hear the case
of Harun al Rashid once again.

Note on Home Office file

Dr Al-Janabi
13-12-2002
fled Iraq – UK
claimed asylum
refused to amputate –
prisoner's hand was healthy
clandestine entry
09-01-2004 –
asylum refused
used false instrument
to enter country.

Domestic worker

Esta Cunha de Silva had watched the rhubarb
erupt through the bare spring garden
like a miniature rainforest.
Now she levered and pulled
and carried in the giant, shuddering canopy
filling the kitchen with sharp, green breath.
As she snapped batons, packed her pie dish,
sheared off curls of crimson veneer,
she heard the screech of falling trees,
the echo of chained timber
moving down the river Solimões Amazonas
taken from her childhood home in Manaus.

With arms full, she flaps out to the compost
twists off the ill-fitting lid and stands back.
A cloud of black gnats billows out
like a clap of dust from the blackboard rubber
in the little school where she'd first heard
the stories of their Opera House –
built by rubber barons
so rich they lit cigars with $100 bills.
Their brazen wealth, like a dormant seed
had germinated within her and in time,
she'd followed the rubber and the timber,
left behind the favelas, the depleted rainforest.

Home Office Files

I feed a fist of papers to the shredder.
It clamps and grips tight.
They buckle rigid and erect
calcified into a frill of coral,
a corrugated shanty town roof.

Stuck, it cannot be moved forward or back.
I pick at compacted paper, bullet hard,
and pull out unravelled spills of typeface,
shreds of Mr Subramanian's life,
his ten years waiting for a decision.

He is still trapped in the chemical stench
of a container pressed down on him
somewhere on the sea fleeing a camp in the Vanni,
his wife and child dead beside him,
prevented from burying them on firm ground.

Nativity

She lay on the sofa
its hard cushions
squashed down into the corner
under the heavy paisley quilt
she'd found there.
There was nothing
left to eat in the fridge,
its door nudged open
swollen with ice,
the fibrous cold
stealing into the room.
Just ice and knots of sweetcorn
heaped in a corner
like rancid yellow straw,
and a bottle of baby milk
left by the Kosovan family
housed there before her.
She'd heard they'd been allowed to stay.
Baby John Harris Farruku
brother to Adriatuk, Flutura and Etmir,
born three days inside the amnesty.
His birth had allowed
the family to begin again
given them the hope
of an ordinary life.

Ali

I have worked
maybe sixty hours this week
in a kitchen in Wembley.
I'll be paid for five.
There is no one to complain to.
They know that.
I could be back in the desert
sweating in this haze
of heat and fear.
And I thought I'd escaped –
those three days
when it reached 54°
too hot to amputate my hand
the blood wouldn't clot.
Bribed a guard and slipped out
into the night sand.
Now I survive
like some phantom limb
aching for what's missing.

Removal Directions

SL authorised a same day removal on this case.

At 6.05 hrs today I attended North Road. Flat D is a top-floor flat above a shop. I obtained entry by speaking to the subject on the intercom. Once in the flat I explained to her that she had no basis to remain in the UK and I had been instructed to detain her in order to effect her removal later that day. I arrested her at 06.20 hrs as a person liable to be detained.

She said it had not come as a surprise and she had been expecting us one day. I then proceeded to get her dressed, escort her to the toilet and then we started packing a suitcase. When bent over taking old things out of the suitcase she appeared faint or dizzy. I told her to kneel on the floor and she sat down and finished packing things laying on her side.

We went to the sitting room to get a photo and then sat down. I said I would not handcuff her if she cooperated. We left the flat but starting to go down the stairs she stopped and sat down. PD and I tried to hold her up and lead her down the stairs but she proceeded to retch and vomit. An ambulance was called. I went with her to the hospital.

She was seen by Dr Bell who declared her fit for detention and flight. He listed all her medication and the dosage. She is on 2 drugs for the HIV, twice daily medication and takes two types of painkillers co-didramol and aspirin. The Dr opined that the shock and anxiety of being deported made her vomit.

At just past 09.00 hrs I advised SL that the subject was fit and well. Arrangements were made for her to be taken direct to IS detention (as team could not get airside). She reported at 11.00 hrs and was handed over with her medication and suitcase. Although nervous and breathing heavily, she said she was feeling OK.

As planned I arrested her under Schedule 2 of IA 1971 and cautioned her. I left her in the care of PL and then proceeded to her address with a search authority signed by CIO. Although no document to assist with removal was found, we collected all the medicines. I also placed the lady's Bible with her medicine that would go with her on the flight.

I informed her that her solicitors were aware of the RDs.

As we promised her, PD and I rang the 2 friends whose numbers she had given us to inform them of the RDs, c15.05 hrs.

Heron Flats

As you push a leaflet through a letterbox
Abdul Rahman dashes out
to petition the case of Xiang Lee
who's been sleeping on his sofa
for the past two years.
You ease off the messenger bag
and sit and take tea with him
on the balcony. You know Abdul,
a serial letter writer in green ink.

He arranges mint leaves in glasses
and you watch them twist and melt
like fur caterpillars, as you sip
on this Sunday afternoon
up here where the North Circular
is constant as the ocean and
next door's finches,
dyed to the colour of flamingos,
squall in their rows of cages.

What you didn't know, was how
hard it was, when he first came
to England in 1964, to get a job
and how many letters he'd written
and how he'd got no replies and then
how, one day, he got an interview
for a position as clerk at TL Holdings –
and how, when he'd got there
he'd found three other candidates
all foreigners like him
and how his boss, Ray Watkins
had taken them all.

Advice Surgery in the Methodist Church Hall

She stares into the vestry mirror
and sees a woman waiting
with two Sainsbury's bags full of papers.
She is wearing a flesh-brown sari
with a long same-coloured cardigan,
the back pulled up by stooped shoulders,
the hem misshapen off the ground.
Under, she sees large, white trainers and black socks.
She sees a woman whose husband was
a diamond-cutting engineer,
now full time in the DFS warehouse.

Below brushed-velvet curtains
the colour of faded bulrushes,
there is a long cupboard for hymn books,
the side door big enough for a child to fit.
She could smell the fruity port of steeped age
in the grand mahogany sideboard with the brass tassels,
her small fingers searching among the forest of panels
for the spring to the drawer
lined with a perfect, green baize lawn.
Remembered how she hid from her fourth cousin,
in the Wadiyar's Palace on a stifling afternoon,
where the fountain splashed dappled light
in the women's courtyard
and the tips of the palms didn't stir,
and tea was served in Windsor china
as they perched on stools
made from huge, wrinkled elephant feet.

The sideboard stretched back into the dark
and she had fallen asleep
in the clunk and clutch of mother of pearl,
and the lingering smell of polished cutlery.
She'd missed the excitement of that afternoon
when a ship had arrived in the docks
carrying a consignment of ball gowns
intended for the Charity Auction, Montgomery, USA.
What a misunderstanding:

instead of a cheque for street orphans
the dresses themselves had arrived.
Coming out of the sideboard,
she saw her Ayah dressed-up in rich taffeta
with hooped petticoats. It was as if
she'd stepped into Confederate Alabama –
bustles and bonnets and fluttering white parasols.
Over the months remnants of those fine clothes
kept turning up on market stalls.

A cold autumn sun filters over
the tashed, grey oak floor
from the high, corded windows,
that lean in to open.
Dried flowers stand in a thick, pleated glass vase
on a white lace altar cloth –
she has been waiting since 5 am
to ask about a visa for her niece –
someone to pass her life on to
who would still understand the sacredness of cows,
who wouldn't put her in a home.

Letters

I would like to express my filling
I love your cuntry
I have applied for neutralisation
My two aunts already restyled in UK
My case is bending with Home Office for long time
My life just waisting away
I was arrested by six uninformed guards
It is wrong under the Court of Commotion of Human Rights
Sir I am sacred

With wormiest regards

Mr Giang

veteran of the American war 1965–1973

Smoke stains the lining of his nose.
He listens to the chime and chink
of riddled barbeque coals
that hover flames
sweeping jagged
when a squirt of lighter fuel
drapes across them.
He watches the casual ease of his grandson
twirling over his knuckle
a cloth of purple flopping meat
as he nonchalantly adjusts the grill
talks animatedly to the guests.

A baseball mitt of steak
is plumped down on his plate,
a pool of red rain collected
in the patchwork leather.
Grampa Giang speaks sixty-two
Vietnamese bird languages,
but in his eighteen years in America
he hasn't yet mastered English.
He concentrates on the words
but as he stretches out to grasp them
they squawk out of reach
disappearing into the haze of mist
that hangs dripping over the rainforest canopy
where the noise of bird song
is louder than a city.

The echolalia of foreign sounds
stutter stubbornly in his throat,
catching on stumps of charred,
defoliated forest
that emit only the ghostly
calling of the gibbons
and the breathless whistles of the birds.

Nursery Tales

Fearful of the dreams she carries
for her unborn child, she feels
the bunch and swoop of her stomach.
She thinks of her grandfather,
a poor Italian immigrant
crossing to America in steerage:
the motion sickness, his stiff cramped limbs
in the hold and the burials at sea from small-pox.
As a small boy, he'd watched on deck
as red hot stones were sewn into greased sheets
and thrown overboard ahead of the bodies
to disperse the circling sharks.
Before poverty and disenchantment had
seared his unsuspecting heart, he had talked
to her of the water, the longing and
waiting, the endless swell of the sea, until
pigeons replaced sea birds. And at
last the sight of Liberty through the mist.

Father

He had finally saved enough
to bring his family to join him;
but DNA tests show that
only two of his three children are his.
The middle one has been refused a visa.

Omnipotence

He'd been bugging me all morning,
phoning insistently
so confident of his rights.
Just wanted the Home Office to hurry up –
but he was bolshie and I snapped.
Told him they were doing further checks,
had called up another file.
Then I heard his voice crumple and go small;
'please don't push them too hard then,
don't make them angry
I'll leave it to time.'

Dr Gopal

She snapped open the kitchen bin
(the maid had forgotten to empty it)
and uncovered a magical world
a sudden frost – like the awe of
seeing her first snowfall in England.
An aubergine had turned old overnight
a shock of white hair standing straight up
on a wizened purple-brown head.
She thought of the plastic trolls
the girls had played with
at her first school in Neasden.
They would brush the long white hair
under their desks as she sat
wriggling in her chair, thick ribbed tights
chaffing her newly enclosed legs
as she waited for the bell.

In Uganda she'd been forbidden dolls,
her mother determined
that she would be educated.
Her Omma had helped her cut
a secret family of paper dolls
which she'd kept hidden under the bed.
But Mama had found the box and burnt them.
She didn't blame her mother.
Now a senior consultant,
she lived the model immigrant life –
with a beautiful house in a quiet street;
but she couldn't stop
the tide of night terrors racing in,
prevent the silhouettes from
curling and peeling in the fires of Entebbe.

Surgery Note 1

His eight year old granddaughter
translates his torrent of angry words.
This senior Afghan KhAD officer
surrounded now by women whose help he needs.
His hands shake with agitation
as he stares through the pattern of words
intricate as a cedar wood screen.

Surgery Note 2

Her documents have been shown and re-shown,
folded back and forwards into a tiny square.
She is flustered as she unpacks her wares,
laying out her flimsy case for asylum
like an old peasant woman
sitting on her shawl in the busy market place
with just one carrot and one potato to sell.

Appeal Judge

Her study is a sanctuary,
like an urban churchyard
under siege from the urgency
of glass and steel,
a last bulwark of justice
for failed asylum seekers
against the ranks of poorly-trained
option-pickers and box-tickers.

Behind the bowed walls of her books,
there is space to consider –
consider with anxious scrutiny –
and wander among the shambling paths
of English case-law
with its accumulation of wisdom,
to admire its elegance,
its balance and proportion
accrued over the years.

Asylum Interview

She has practised the safe phrases —
'I passed through unknown countries.'
'Agent took my passport.'
Even in her broken English
she says only what will help her case.
But the sides of the path are mined
and he is waiting for her to slip.

Her skin sweats.
Catarrh is blocked solid in her nose.
She shunts and pulls to try to move it.
One nostril clears momentarily
a messy clank of iron and locks
rattling and unfastening.
'Why have you claimed asylum?'
She sneezes and apologises.
'I have a cold.'
He writes this down.

She is trying to protect herself
but she has no energy.
He fires questions at her in bursts.
His pen scores the paper
drawing back her cover
like a soft flap of mango skin
exposing her shame,
beating yolk orange like a fontanel.
He has realised the truth
but doesn't correct his notes —
raped by soldiers of the Lord's Resistance Army:
her immune system has been shot through,
her CD4 count a mere six cells.

New email address

LuckyinUK_@netnet.com

Promise

I recognise Promise, waiting.
Sick and homeless
her problems are compounded
by the threat of deportation.
Her surgery form is tucked
into the Hello magazine she is reading.

When I was sick and a child, my father
would bring me home a comic
slipped inside his newspaper.
I would wait through the long day
flushed and feverish
in the silent house.

In the evening he would stoop
out of the car, his folded paper
pressed against his tan attaché case
with the dark hand stain.
He smelt of office
and undisclosed anxieties.

I would look for the comic's bright
splash of promise that gilded
the dampened flannel of newsprint
that cloaked my father's shoulders
in the world's injustices,
too big then for me to comprehend.

Chance

Chance he was in this queue,
rather than that.
Chance that his brother
joined a different one
and was granted leave
when he was refused.
Chance he had left the house
when the militia came.
Chance his wife had been killed
queuing for a visa.

Stamps

Dad's receptionist saved stamps for us
which he brought home in a bulging
rolled over manila envelope.
We would shake the packet out over the floor
and take it in turns to bargain
for the blackly franked blocks of four;
lions from Rhodesia & Nyasaland
women tea-pickers in Ceylon
a single green triangular one.

I would cut round the stamps
allowing a small margin of envelope
and float them on a bowl of water
carried slopping from the sink.
I'd leave them to soak until their sleek, gluey backs
peeled away then lay them to dry on a towel
before lifting them from the rough weave
by their curled perforated edge
to press under heavy books.

These were the stamps we fought over;
not the flimsy cellophane cards of mint sets
that swivelled on stands shaped like Christmas trees
while my mother queued at the back of
the shop for the post office counter.
Not the pristine cream-backed stamps
the postmaster would ease apart
from the dropped down folded slats
in his maroon ledger.
We wanted the ones
that had made the journey;
that bore the marks of their struggle.

GLOSSARY OF ABBREVIATIONS

A = Asylum
AA = Administrative Assistant,
ABS = Absconder
i- Cm = Asylum Cases Information Database.
ACC = Accompanying
ACU = Asylum Co-ordination Uni
ADJ = Adjudicator.
AEA = Alter Entry Appeals.
AFB = Asylum Fingerprint Bureau
AfU = Application Ferrrs Unit.
AG = Asylum Group.
A. = Asylum Immigration
ATO = Assistant Immigration Offio
A-R = Asylum Interview Record
AIT = Asylum and Immigration Tribunal
ALV = Asylum Liaison Unit.
AN = Application for Naturalisatio
.oq = Administrative Officer
APC = Appeals processing Centre
APP = Application
APU = Asylum Policy Unit
AR C = Asylum Registration Care.
ARE = Appeal Rights Exhausted
ASS = Appeals Support Section
ASU = Asylum Screening Unit.
ASY = Asylum
AS YS = Asylum Support System
AVR = Assisted Voluntary Returns
Bep! = Border Control Policy Implementation.
BCU = Business Case Unit.
BEG = Bedford Enforcement Office
Cfl. = Call No
CCT = Criminal Casework Team /
Complex Case work Team
CEU = Croydon Enforcement Unit
Cir: = Case I   Database
CiO = Chief Immigration Officer.
eLN = Clandestine
CM j = Casework Management Un
COA = Change of Address.
CPC = Central Point of Contact
CPS = Crown Prosecution Unit.
CrU = Computer Records Immigration Service Hybrid / Computer Records immigration Service Investigation Section
CVIK. = Casework
DC = Detention Centre
DEMPU = Detainee Escorting & Population Management Unit.
DEP = Dependant.
(D)EU = (Dover) Enforcement Unit.
DL = Discretionary Leave
DMC = Document Management Centr
DR = Detention Review.
EA = Emergency Accommodation.
EAS = Existing Asylum Seeker
EC = Entry Clearance.
ECO = Entry Clearance Officer.
EOD = Enforcement Distribution Desk
EDR = Expected Date of Release
EEA = European Economic Area
ELR = Exceptional Leave to Remain.
ELTE / XLTE = Exceptional Leave to Enter.
EME = East Midlands Enforcement
ERCU = Enforcement and Removals Caseworking Unit
EY = Emergency Voucher.
EV's = Emergency Vouchers.

EXTN = Extension.
F AO = For Attention Of
F AS = Failed Asylum Seeker
FLR = Further Leave to Remain.
For = Freedom of Information,
FR = Final Refusal
fTR = Failure To Report.
fTS = File Tracking System
F1T = Failure to Travel.
G = General
GAT = Gatwick.
GCID = General Cases Infonnatic Database.
GOA = Grounds of Appeal.
HAT = Housing + Accommodatio Team,
He = High Commission.
HEO = Higher Executive Officer
HMI = Her Majesty's Inspector
HO = Home Office
HR = Human Rights.
ISMP = Highly Skilled Migrant Program
iff = in time! In Transit
.fly = Interview.
IAA = Immigration Appellant Authority.
IAF = Immigration Asylum Finqeq
BU = Interview Booking Unit.
ICe = Initial Consideration Croydo
ICD = Integrated Casework Directc
OJ = Initial Consideration Unit.
IES = Illegal Entry Section.
IFB = Immigration Fingerprint Bun
I.I = Illegal
iMM = Immigration
NDCS = Immigration Directorate Electronic System
INER = Immigration Nau   ity Enquiry Bureau.
NT = Interview
= immigration Officer.
= Immigration Service.
SDU = Immigration Service Documentation Unit
SHQ = Immigration Service headquarters.
LC = Landing Card
LcU = Landing Card Unit.
doO = Local Enforcement Office.
LHR = London Heathrow.
LKA = Last Known Address
LSCU = London Support Casework Unit.
TE = Leave to Enter.
TR = Leave to Remain.
WT = London Workflow Team.
Vi/Celt = Marriage Certificate.
Vi CT = Ministerial Correspondence Unil
MEU = Midlands Enforcement Unit
MODCU = Management of Detained Cases Unit.
MOE = Method Of Entry
PCS = Ministerial Correspondence Section.
PO = MP's Office
= Nationality
SS = National Asylum Support Service.
T = National
C = Non Charging Casework.
3 = Nationality Directorate.

NFA = Further Action
NK = Known
NP = Political Asylum.
NST = ional Support Team
NTL = Time Limit.
N/A = Applicable
OOT = of Time Application.
OPR = er Ports Removal
OSCU = serational Support & Certifi.   Unit
PA = P   al Asylum
PAS = Administration System
PAX = senger,
PCU = ic Caller Unit
PEO = ic Enquiry Office.
PO = ling Officer
POA = of Arrival! Proof of Address
POU = nting Officers Unit.
PPT = f   ort.
PR = Pc   Registration .
PROFFI = Private Office
PTA = Tribunal Appeal.
R = Ref
RC = ft   ing Centre.
RCT = vals and Cessation's Team.
RCU = ua! Casework Unit.
RD = al Directions.
REPS = esematives
RESCU = movals Strategy and Co-ordinate
RFRL = it
RG = Re   ons For Refusal Letter.
RIF = Re   ils Group.
R = e Index Form
ROA = Leave to Enter.
RIE = of Appeal.
RP = ce Permi
RE = of Passp
RE = Rep   gration.
RS = Reg   SUpport.
RST = Rs   als & Cessations Team.
RV = R't   Vouchers.
S ofS = tary of State .
SAG = St   ent of Additional Grounds.
SiU = St.   d Acknowledgement Letter.
SEF = St3   nt of Evidence Form
ST = SUPI   Token.
SIU = Sh
St lB = Su   tence.
SUBS = S   rhone call.
T/r.AT.T = ry Admission.
TA = Tel11   spatcher.
TD = Tem   l 2 Heathrow.
TN2 = Tm   yRelease.
TR = Tern   companied Asylum
VASC = L   Seeking C,   en
UK = Unil   ingdom
UKPA = t   j Kingdom Passport Agency.
UNHCR = ed Nations High Commissic   r Refugees
VAF = Vi   plication Form.
VARP = V   tary Assisted Returns Programm
VL = Vouc   clter
WDW = Vi   awn
WIP = wo   Holidaymaker Progress.
WP = Worl   mit.
XFR = Tra: red
XLTR = E: ional Leave to Remain.

Acknowledgements

Thank you to the editors of the following publications where some of these poems first appeared: *Poetry Review, Orbis, The North, Agenda, Theology Journal, Whispers in Smoke (Anthology) Soaring Penguin Press, Say Cheese! A book of happy poems (Anthology) Rookhurst Press.*

The Scarlet Lizard was a prize winner in The Troubadour Poetry Competition 2012. *Teenager* was a prize winner in The Troubadour Poetry Competition 2013. *Brook Court* was commended in The Second Light Poetry Competition 2014. *Spouse Visa* was shortlisted in the Bridport Poetry Competition 2014. *Luck* was shortlisted in the Bridport Poetry Competition 2015.

Special thanks to Ann, Edwina, Val, Gill, Kate, Anita and Jolyne for all their constructive advice and friendship at Poets Meeting. Amy Wack has been a hugely supportive editor and I would like to thank her and all at Seren for their encouragement and meticulous work. Thanks are also due to The Nehru Centre, 8 South Audley Street, London W1K 1HF (www.nehru-centre.org.uk) which has kindly been provided for our book launch by The Indian High Commission.

Most of all I would like to thank the resilient and inspiring people who fill the pages of this book.